OVERCOMING

OVER-COMING

BY RICK YOHN

Dahlgren Methodist Church
Dahlgren, Virginia 22448

A MINISTRY OF THE NAVIGATORS
P.O. Box 6000, Colorado Springs, Colorado 80934

The Navigators is an international, evangelical Christian organization. Jesus Christ gave His followers the Great Commission to go and make disciples (Matthew 28:19). The aim of The Navigators is to help fulfill that commission by multiplying laborers for Christ in every nation.

NavPress is the publishing ministry of The Navigators. NavPress publications are tools to help Christians grow. Although publications alone cannot make disciples or change lives, they can help believers learn biblical discipleship, and apply what they learn to their lives and ministries.

© 1985 by Rick Yohn
All rights reserved, including translation
Library of Congress Catalog Card Number: 84-61529
ISBN: 0-89109-055-X
10553

Second printing, 1985

Cover illustration: Marcus Hamilton

Unless otherwise identified, Scripture quotations are from the *Holy Bible: New International Version.* © Copyright 1973, 1978, 1984 New York International Bible Society. Used by permission of Zondervan Publishers. Also used is the *New American Standard Bible,* © The Lockman Foundation 1960, 1962, 1963, 1968, 1971, 1972, 1973, 1975, 1977.

Printed in the United States of America

CONTENTS

How to Use this Study 7
1 Identifying the Enemy 9
2 The Battle of Deception 19
3 The Battle of Discouragement—Its Causes 31
4 The Battle of Discouragement—Its Cure 41
5 The Battle of Covetousness 53
6 The Battle of Physical Impairment 63
7 The Battle of Selfishness 71
8 What Are My Resources? 83

HOW TO USE THIS STUDY

TAKE TIME TO PREPARE YOURSELF
1. Preview the entire booklet. Leaf through the pages, noting the boldfaced headings, the arrangement of the materials, and the general goal of the lessons.
2. As you approach each lesson, preview it, and read its introduction and conclusion. You will comprehend and retain more if you know where the study is going. When you finish a lesson, mark the highlights with stars and anything unclear with a question mark.
3. Before you begin your next lesson, review the previous one, giving special attention to the stars and question marks. You will be amazed that questioned areas may seem clear this time.
4. Pray before and after you study for insight into the Scriptures, for willingness to respond to God's truth, and for wisdom in how to apply His truth to your life.

RECOGNIZE YOUR RESOURCES
1. The Holy Spirit (1 John 2:28)
2. The Scriptures (2 Timothy 3:6-17)
3. Mature Believers
    a. Gifted teachers (1 Corinthians 12:28)
    b. Encouragers (Hebrews 10:24-25, 1 Thessalonians 5:11)
    c. Those who are gifted at pulling the best from you (Proverbs 20:5)
4. This study guide

FOR PERSONAL STUDY (2 Timothy 2:15)
1. Select a specific time each day when you are the most alert for study. Do everything possible to keep the same hour.
2. Don't feel compelled to complete the entire lesson at one sitting. You may want to divide the longer lessons into two parts. You decide the natural break.
3. Avoid letting your time spent in this Bible study become a mere academic exercise. Remember that you are interacting with God's life-changing Word (1 Corinthians 8:1, Hebrews 4:12).
4. After the lesson ask yourself how the information has made a change in your attitude, behavior and understanding.

FOR ONE-ON-ONE STUDY (Proverbs 27:17)
1. Ask the Lord for one person with whom you could share yourself. It could be someone who could help you grow spiritually and/or one whom you could encourage.
2. Decide together on the best time and location for your study.
3. Be willing to be vulnerable and transparent. Remove masks and refuse to develop defense systems.
4. Let the study change you as well as the other person.

FOR GROUP STUDY (2 Timothy 2:2)
Recognize that in a small group you have special dynamics which are different from personal or one-on-one study. They include different personalities, backgrounds, interests, occupations, degree of spiritual maturity, etc. Some members will not want to share their opinions, while others will want to dominate the discussion. The group should encourage discussion from each member.

Take time at the beginning of each meeting to review the previous lesson and to share God's blessings from the past week. Then the group leader should focus attention on the first few questions of the new lesson. He may also give some of his own reactions to the lesson. If the group is large, it should break into smaller groups to work on the lesson and then reassemble at the end to share discoveries.

CHAPTER ONE
IDENTIFYING THE ENEMY

In his book *How Come It's Taking Me So Long to Get Better?* Dr. Lane Adams views the Christian life as a military campaign. First, there is the *invasion of enemy-held territory*, and then the *establishing of the beachhead.*

According to the Scriptures, each of us is like an enemy-held island, cut off from the land mass. Paul describes this life of isolation as he writes, "remember that at that time you were separate from Christ, excluded from citizenship in Israel and foreigners to the covenants of the promise, without hope and without God in the world" (Ephesians 2:12). That's isolation!

Continuing to describe our situation, Paul says, "you were dead in your transgressions and sins, in which you used to live when you followed the ways of this world and of *the ruler of the kingdom of the air, the spirit* who is now at work in those who are disobedient" (Ephesians 2:1-2). What is the apostle implying with these words? He is informing his readers that a spirit used to have powerful influence over our lives, keeping us in spiritual darkness. But then another Spirit invaded us from outside. Paul explains this event, writing, "But because of His great love for us, God, who is rich in mercy, made us alive with Christ even when we were dead in transgressions—it is by grace you have been saved" (Ephesians 2:4-5).

Conversion! That was the time of God's invasion. And who was that other Spirit? He was God's Holy Spirit, who entered our lives and set the stage for the battle of life. Now that God has established a beachhead in your life,

His Holy Spirit is capturing the entire island, a little at a time.

This conquest—the believer's growth into sanctification (holiness of character)—will include a lifetime of battles and conflicts. Does this mean that we receive more of the Holy Spirit? Not at all. Rather, He receives more of us as we little by little turn over to Him our spiritual lives, finances, morals, ambitions, plans, fears, family, jobs, hidden secrets to which we cling, unhealthy habits, wrong desires, doubts, and many other areas.

As we turn over these areas to God's Spirit, the warfare rages, for the enemy has a strong foothold and does not give up easily (Ephesians 6:12). So we fight. Sometimes we feel as though everything is lost. We feel defeated, discouraged, and disgusted with ourselves. We fight the same battles over and over, and we may even lose more battles than we win in our early years after conversion.

But there is good news. The enemy has been defeated. The war has already been won by our commander-in-chief, Jesus Christ. However, victory is ours only when we yield each of our struggles to Christ, letting Him live and act through us. As we fight the battles with God's strategy and strength, we win. When we attempt to fight the enemy in our own strength, using our own strategies, we lose.

So begin now to win the war battle by battle by first unmasking your adversary. In this chapter you will discover the enemy's nature, location, strengths, and weaknesses.

YOUR ENEMY'S NATURE
Do you really know whom you are up against? Listen to Paul's vivid description: "For our struggle is not against flesh and blood, but against the rulers, against the authorities, against the powers of this world and against the spiritual forces of evil in the heavenly realms" (Ephesians 6:12).

Your battle is against spiritual beings who are led by Satan himself. But who is Satan? Some amusing red elf who stokes the coals of hell with his cute pitchfork? Certainly not. Who could be afraid of a creature like that? Is Satan a mere force of evil, or is he a being with a personality? Is he ugly or beautiful? A myth or a reality?

1. List everything you now believe about Satan. Try to describe him in five words or phrases.

   a. _____

   b. _____

   c. _____

   d. _____

   e. _____

2. Circle the phrase in each pair below which you think best describes him.

   a. impersonal force   created being

   b. harmful   harmless

   c. beautiful   ugly

   d. in hell   out of hell

   e. all powerful   limited in power

   f. more intelligent   less intelligent
      than man   than man

   Now that you have stimulated your thinking about this enemy, check your views against the teachings of the Old and New Testaments.

3. Isaiah 14:3-23 is a prophecy against the king of Babylon. However, as Isaiah prophesied, he saw through the earthly king to the power behind him. The prophet's vision shifted back and forth.

   a. In 14:12, what name did Isaiah say was this power's before he sinned?

   _____

   b. From Isaiah 14:13-14, explain Lucifer's (Latin for "light-bearer") sin.

   _____
   _____
   _____

4. Ezekiel had a similar experience of seeing the spiritual enemy behind an earthly king. Ezekiel 28:1-19 is a prophecy condemning the king of Tyre, but 28:11-19 addresses the evil one himself.

   a. Describe Lucifer before his fall (28:11-15).

   _____

   _____

   _____

   The cherubim are an order of angels. Cherubim flanked the atonement cover (KJV: mercy seat), the symbolic throne of God in the temple's Holy of Holies (Exodus 25:18-22). Lucifer was in Eden to serve or instruct the first humans (Ezekiel 28:13), and after they sinned other cherubim were appointed to guard holy Eden and the tree of life from fallen men's return (Genesis 3:24). "Guardian" in Ezekiel 28:14 and 16 equally means "one who covers," for the cherubim covered God's throne with their wings, shielding and proclaiming His glory. For Ezekiel's vision of unfallen cherubim, see Ezekiel 10.

   b. What was Lucifer created to be and do?

   _____

   _____

   _____

   c. Lucifer was the greatest among the greatest class of created beings. From Ezekiel 28:15-18, describe each aspect of his sin.

   _____

   _____

   _____

   _____

   _____

d. How did God respond (28:15-19)?

e. What lesson can you draw from Lucifer's attitude toward the nature and purpose God had ordained for him? Why does his sin lie at the root of all sin?

5. Since his fall, the titles "Lucifer" and "son of the dawn" have been stripped from the enemy, yet now he has many other names. After each of the following cross-references, write what the name it gives reveals about him.

Matthew 12:24-27, *Beelzebub, the prince of demons*

Mark 4:13-15, *Satan* (Resister, Adversary)

2 Corinthians 6:15, *Belial* (Worthlessness)

Revelation 9:11, *Abadon, Apollyon* (Destroyer)

Revelation 12:9, *the ancient serpent called the devil*

Revelation 12:10, *the accuser of our brothers*

At this point you should be aware that you are not fighting some harmless creature or the figment of someone's imagination. Satan is real. But where does he live?

YOUR ENEMY'S LOCATION
One of the most successful strategies of warfare is the ambush. The enemy camouflages himself and waits for the unsuspecting victim to pass by. Unaware of his enemy's nearness, the soldier is entrapped. Likewise, a person who thinks that Satan lives in hell and is not loose on the earth will receive many surprises.

6. a. For whom was hell ("the eternal fire") prepared (Matthew 25:41)?

   b. Revelation 20 describes the events surrounding Christ's second coming. From 20:1-3 and 7-10, describe what will happen to Satan at that time.

   c. By implication, then, where is Satan now, and where is he not?

7. Where do Ephesians 2:2 and 6:12 say Satan is?

8. a. According to Job 1:6, where does Satan go, and why?

b. How can you reconcile these facts with Ezekiel's prophecy that Satan was banished from heaven?

_____

_____

_____

_____

9. a. Where else does Satan go, and what does he do there (Job 1:7)?

_____

_____

b. Explain in your own words how Peter describes Satan's activity (1 Peter 5:8).

_____

_____

_____

The devil uses his access to this planet to do everything he can to lead people away from personal relationships with God. He will try to make you "good" by human standards or "religious" if he can thereby prevent you from coming to the cross for forgiveness of sin.

But your enemy's nature and location are only part of the information you need to win the battles. Consider also his strengths and weaknesses.

YOUR ENEMY'S STRENGTHS AND WEAKNESSES

10. Over what four areas of life does Satan exercise power?

    Job 1:12,14-15,19 _____

    Matthew 13:19 _____

    Luke 8:27-29,35 _____

    Luke 13:11 _____

11. Describe how you or someone you know has experienced Satan's activity in one of these areas.

12. What limits to Satan's power do Job 1:12 and 2:6 reveal?

13. According to Colossians 1:15-16, why was Christ greater than Satan even before His incarnation and crucifixion?

14. Remember that Satan is your adversary, your accuser, the witness against you in God's court of justice. Why did Christ's death on the cross utterly defeat Satan (Colossians 1:21-22, 2 Corinthians 5:21)?

15. How can you let that defeat become real in your experience (Colossians 1:23, James 4:7)?

Moreover, Satan predicted that Job would curse God if He allowed Job to be tested, and yet Job did not curse God. Therefore, the devil is limited in his knowledge. He may think that he knows how men will react under specific circumstances, but he does not have that foreknowledge. Furthermore, since Satan had to leave Earth to go before God (Job 1:7, 2:2), he cannot be present everywhere at the same time. Only God is everywhere at once; Satan is a created being. Therefore, Satan must send one of his lieutenant demons to persecute most people.

You have been drafted into a spiritual warfare. Whether you want to fight or not, you are involved in spiritual battles every day of your life. The questions you need to answer for yourself are: Do I know my enemy well enough to win the battle? Do I care whether I can defeat him? Am I willing to pay the price of victory?

You have captured just a glimpse of your enemy. In the following chapters of this book you will study the many battlefields on which you will engage him. Your job is to understand these fields and to discover how you can win the war, battle by battle.

CHAPTER TWO
THE BATTLE OF DECEPTION

At the beginning of the football season, each team enters the competition with hundreds of new plays. As the season progresses, the coaches evaluate which plays work and which need to be altered or discarded altogether. Some basic strategies work most of the time against opponents. These plays become the basic strategies of each game.

In the last chapter you discovered that you are in a spiritual warfare. Your enemy is a rebellious angel of God who roams around earth, attempting to ruin the lives of men and women, teenagers and children. He uses some basic strategies that have worked over the years to keep unbelievers from coming into personal relationships with Christ and to hinder the spiritual growth of Christians.

The apostle Paul challenged the Ephesian believers, "Put on the full armor of God so that you can take your stand against the devil's *schemes*" (Ephesians 6:11). The word translated "schemes" is the Greek word *methodeias*, from which we derive the term *methods*. The enemy has a vast arsenal of methods in reserve to use against you.

Another word used in Paul's second letter to the Corinthians has a similar connotation. Paul pronounced forgiveness "in order that Satan might not outwit us. For we are not unaware of his schemes" (2 Corinthians 2:11). Here the Greek word means "purpose" or "design."

Just as God loves you and has a wonderful plan for your life, so Satan hates you and has designed a miserable plan for your life. He will use every trick and scheme of his imagination to entrap you, to make you a victim of his plan. Therefore, in the next chapters you will investigate some of these schemes, in order to better understand the battlefields on which the enemy wages war against you.

Consider in this chapter the battlefield of deception—where fighting occurs concerning business, politics, marriage, religion, and so on. Deceit attempts to hide reality. It covers up the truth and projects a fabricated story as truth. Prepare to confront your arch-enemy on the field of deception, and learn to win the battle there.

SATAN IS YOUR ARCH-DECEIVER

1. a. What deception did Paul fear would befall the Corinthians (2 Corinthians 11:3)?

   _____

   _____

   b. What trait of the Corinthians prompted this concern (2 Corinthians 11:4)?

   _____

   _____

2. The New Testament specifically warns against deception in four places. Explain the deception against which Paul and James warned in each of the following verses.

   1 Corinthians 6:9-10 _____

   _____

   1 Corinthians 15:33 _____

   _____

   Galatians 6:7 _____

   _____

   James 1:16-18 _____

   _____

3. Describe an occasion on which you have been tempted to believe one of these lies.

_____
_____
_____
_____
_____

Though Satan is the one who deceives people, he uses various channels to accomplish his purpose. He would never appear to you as some grotesque monster and tell you to sin against God. That would be too obvious. You would never fall for it. Hence, he disguises himself and works behind the scenes, appealing to your physical, emotional, intellectual, and spiritual senses.

4. According to James 1:14-15, what about you makes you easily deceived?

_____
_____
_____
_____

5. From the verses below, note some of the channels through which the devil can deceive. Note also how you cooperate with him.

Deuteronomy 11:16 _____
_____

Psalm 50:19 _____
_____

Proverbs 31:30 _____
_____

Jeremiah 49:16 (To a Hebrew, the heart was the deepest seat of will, emotions, and intellect. In it were his motives, his goals, his assumptions.)

Mark 4:19 _____

Romans 16:18 _____

Hebrews 3:13 (How is sin deceitful?) _____

6. Write examples of how Satan has used two of these means to deceive you.

   a. _____

   b. _____

Scripture records many of Satan's deceptions, but the outstanding example is his deception of Eve. As you read in Genesis 3:1-7 the account of the first deception in history, observe how subtly the plan of deceit unfolded.

THE SERPENT
Today many people fear snakes and reptiles of any kind. But Eve had nothing to fear. No one had ever died. There

was no danger of being bitten, strangled, or harmed in any way by the serpent. Adam himself had named all of the animals. They were all in subjection to him. So for a serpent to approach Eve without inspiring fear was natural. It was as unthreatening as when your own pet dog approaches you, wagging his tail.

7. a. What deception did Paul say in 2 Corinthians 11:14 was usual for Satan?

   _____

   b. Why did Paul give this warning (11:13-15)?

   _____
   _____
   _____

8. What character qualities does the Bible give to serpents?

   Genesis 3:1 _____

   Genesis 49:17 _____

   Psalm 58:3-4 _____

   Micah 7:17 _____

9. Select one of those qualities (besides deception) and describe how Satan is like a serpent.

   _____
   _____
   _____

10. State the first tactic in Satan's plan to deceive Eve.

    _____
    _____

THE GARDEN

The devil came to Eve. She was not tempted in a foreign land, in unfamiliar surroundings. She was tempted at home. Everything was familiar.

11. a. What is Satan's second principle of deceit?

   b. How might he apply it in assailing you?

THE QUESTION

12. a. What *exactly* did God command Adam (Genesis 2:16-17)?

   b. How did the serpent quote God (Genesis 3:1)?

   c. What effect upon Eve was this question meant to produce?

A couple who decides to live together may justify their action by raising the question, "Has God said that sex is wrong?" If you answer, "No," they may then reply, "Well, all we're doing is fulfilling the desires which God has given us in the first place." A clever way of trying to remove guilt is by denying the fact that immorality greatly offends the holiness and purity of God's character.

Just as God never said that eating from *any* tree is wrong, neither did He ever imply that *all* sexual relationships are wrong. But by planting doubt in Eve's mind, the enemy established a beachhead, preparing for a frontal assault.

13. Why was death the inevitable consequence of violating God's command?

14. Do you think the command and the penalty were fair? Why or why not?

THE LIE
At this point the deception moved from planting doubt to an outright lie.

15. a. What part of God's command did the enemy deny (Genesis 3:2-4)?

   b. Compare John 3:16. What in that verse do people often deny?

   c. How did Jesus describe the devil in John 8:44?

People do not like to think in terms of paying a penalty. Society conditions us either to ignore life's penalties, telling us that we will be exceptions to the rule, or to deny that a penalty exists.

The law requires the tobacco industry to place a warning on packages of cigarettes that smoking can be dangerous to your health. Still, people continue to smoke. Tell a parent that his permissive child-rearing will reap devastating results in the future, and he will just smile knowingly and continue to give his children all the freedom they want. Warn a man who is having an affair that there is a tremendous price tag on his weeks or months of pleasure, and he will tell you that he has everything under control.

THE ACCUSATION

Next Satan went a step further in his clever game—he questioned God's purpose.

16. How did the enemy imply that God was trying to take all the fun out of life (Genesis 3:5)?

___

___

___

Today he tells Christians, "If you give in to God, He'll send you to Africa as a missionary." "You'll never be able to make any money." "You'll always be narrow-minded and miserable."

17. Of what does he accuse God to you?

___

___

___

___

THE TEMPTATION

The devil let Eve's own lust for pleasure, perhaps with some encouragement, do the rest (Genesis 3:6). Have you ever seen commercials for alcohol which show the winos, the highway deaths, the broken marriages, and the lost jobs which result from drinking? Absolutely not. You see only Mr. Macho with his can of beer and Miss Sophisticated with her glass of wine. This is how the enemy works. He emphasizes the pleasure and ignores the tragic consequences.

- The Enemy Focuses on What Gives Instant Physical Satisfaction
- The Enemy Focuses on What is Beautiful
- The Enemy Focuses on What Feeds the Ego

"... good for food ... pleasing to the eye ... desirable for gaining wisdom...."

18. How have you experienced these temptations in the last few days?

THE RESULTS
Not only did Satan lead Eve into sin through deception, he enjoyed a second victory when she shared the fruit with her husband.

19. a. How did Paul describe the devastating results of this deception in Romans 5:12?

   b. Why did Adam and Eve's sin produce such consequences for their descendants?

20. Explain God's solution to this problem (Romans 5:17).

_____

_____

WINNING THE BATTLE
Can deception be avoided? Is there a way by which you can win the battle over deception? Definitely! How? The first step, of course, is to become aware that the battle is raging:

First, be aware that the battle exists.

Second, protect your blind side.

The enemy will always come against you on your blind side, like the lineman who circles the quarterback who is concentrating on throwing the touchdown pass. Pow! The quarterback is sacked.

21. Jesus often referred to the Pharisees as blind leaders of the blind. To what were they blind?

    Matthew 6:1-2,5,16 _____

    _____

    Matthew 23:13 _____

    Matthew 23:23-24 _____

    Matthew 23:27-28 _____

    Luke 16:11-15 _____

    Luke 18:10-14 _____

22. In which of these areas do you tend to be blind. Explain how.

    _____

    _____

    _____

    _____

    _____

Third, gain a working knowledge of the truth.

23. List several ways in which you can gain knowledge of the truth.

   a. Luke 11:13, John 14:26 _____

   _____

   b. Hebrews 4:12 _____

   c. _____

24. What is the danger of just accumulating knowledge (1 Corinthians 8:1)?

   _____

   _____

Fourth, use the knowledge you gain in everyday life

Eve's problem was not ignorance of truth. It was her neglect of applying the truth. God's word is a reservoir of truth about spiritual living, money management, family relationships, moral standards, pure and impure motives, and so on. However, unless you put its principles to work in your life, it is as useless as an unplugged lamp in a dark room.

25. How did James describe this step (James 1:22)?

   _____

26. a. How did John describe this step (1 John 3:18)?

   _____

   b. What example did he give (1 John 3:17)?

   _____

   _____

CONCLUSION

You now have gained some understanding of the enemy's first strategy which he used successfully against Eve. Because this method has always been so successful, it remains one of Satan's basic tools for ruining lives. Therefore, whether you like it or not, you will be involved in this battle. And the best weapon which you can use against your enemy in this arena is "the sword of the Spirit, which is the word of God" (Ephesians 6:17).

YOUR RESPONSE

27. What one basic truth or lesson have you learned in this chapter?

   _____
   _____
   _____
   _____

28. Describe the course of action you will take in order to win the battle of deception.

   _____
   _____
   _____
   _____
   _____
   _____
   _____
   _____

CHAPTER THREE
THE BATTLE OF DISCOURAGEMENT—ITS CAUSES

Moses: the great deliverer of the nation Israel; the only one in his time who spoke face to face with God; the fearless lawgiver; the faithful servant of God; the most humble man of his day. Because Moses exhibited such character and success in his life, we tend to forget those human frailties which seeped through his magnificent reputation—character traits such as self-doubt (Exodus 3:11), disorganization (Exodus 18:13-23), disobedience (Numbers 20:8-13), and one which almost defeated him—discouragement.

The Book of Numbers records a moment when he almost lost this battle. The Lord wanted to bring Israel into the promised land. He had faithfully provided for the people's needs with manna. But they wanted more—they craved meat. Their complaints angered the Lord and so discouraged Moses that he was ready to throw in the towel.

Listen to Moses' discouraged cry to God:

> Why have you brought this trouble on your servant? What have I done to displease you that you put the burden of all these people on me? Did I conceive all these people? Did I give them birth? Why do you tell me to carry them in my arms, as a nurse carries an infant, to the land you promised on oath to their forefathers? Where can I get meat for all these people? They keep wailing to me, "Give us meat to eat!" I cannot carry all these people by myself; the burden is too heavy for me. If this is how you are going to treat me,

put me to death right now—if I have found favor in your eyes—and do not let me face my own ruin (Numbers 11:11-15).

Moses had had enough. He was through. "Lord, I give up! I don't even want to live any longer. I don't care if we never get to the promised land!"

Ever feel like that? I have, over the years of my ministry. I have wanted to quit. I have wanted to tell people what I thought of them. I have told myself, "I don't need this. I'll go somewhere else where I might be appreciated more."

But as Dr. V. Raymond Edman, former President of Wheaton College, used to say, "It's always too soon to quit." If you are discouraged at this moment, don't throw in the towel. Study this chapter and discover how God can help you win the battle of discouragement to the point where you not only experience a new power and joy in your life, but even become an encourager of others.

Why do we sometimes get so discouraged? What circumstances contribute to our feelings of giving up?

FEAR BREEDS DISCOURAGEMENT

1. Explain the reason for discouragement in each of the following passages.

   Numbers 13:31-33 _____

   Ezra 4:[1-3]4-6 _____

   Nehemiah 6:[1-4]5-9 _____

2. List three fears which have tempted you to discouragement.

   a. _____
   b. _____
   c. _____

Besides your own fear, other people's fear can also discourage you. Israel refused to enter the promised land because ten of the twelve spies were afraid to face the opposition in the land (Numbers 32:6-9). When leaders become fearful, those who follow them will also grow discouraged. Another cause of discouragement is failure.

FAILURE MAY LEAD TO DISCOURAGEMENT

When Moses was first asked to go to Egypt and confront Pharaoh, he made every excuse he could think of why it would not work. Finally, he accepted God's commission and headed for Egypt. But Moses and Aaron's first attempt met a brick wall. Pharaoh refused to heed their request, had Israel's foremen beaten, maintained the quota of bricks, and even ordered the Israelites to find their own straw with which to make the bricks.

Notice the responses of both the foremen and the two brothers to this colossal failure.

> When they [the foremen] left Pharaoh, they found Moses and Aaron waiting to meet them, and they said, "May the Lord look upon you and judge you! You have made us a stench to Pharaoh and his servants and have put a sword in their hand to kill us." Moses returned to the Lord and said, "O Lord, why have you brought trouble upon this people? Is this why you sent me? Ever since I went to Pharaoh to speak in your name, he has brought trouble upon this people, and you have not rescued your people at all" (Exodus 5:20-23).

3. Name a failure in the past that caused you to be discouraged.

_____

_____

_____

_____

4. How did you attempt to cope with your failure and discouragement?

_____

_____

5. a. On a scale of one to ten (ten the highest), how would you rate your success in handling that discouragement? (Circle one)

   1   2   3   4   5   6   7   8   9   10

   b. Why?

   _____

   _____

   _____

   _____

6. God answered Moses' prayer, but deliverance for Israel was not immediate. Why did God delay the deliverance (Exodus 11:9)?

   _____

   _____

7. Is this reason relevant to your example in question 3? Explain. How did God use your failure?

   _____

   _____

   _____

   _____

   _____

    Fear and failure are primary causes of discouragement. You could also add feelings of inadequacy, temperament, bad news, and tragedy. But a common cause of depression and discouragement is sin. David was entrapped by its tentacles.

SIN MAY LEAD TO DISCOURAGEMENT
David's sin of immorality with Bathsheba led him to pour out his heart to God in two psalms.

8. a. Read Psalm 32:1-5. How did David feel before he confessed his sin? Why?

   b. How did he feel after he confessed it? Why?

9. a. Read Psalm 51. For what did David long?

   Verse 8 _____

   Verse 12 _____

   b. What promises did he make to God?

   Verse 13 _____

   Verse 14 _____

   Verse 15 _____

10. Why does sin foster discouragement?

Besides fear, failure, and sin, personal affliction and trials also breed discouragement. The Scriptures record many afflictions of God's servants.

AFFLICTION MAY CAUSE DISCOURAGEMENT

Jesus promised his disciples that in this world they would experience affliction (John 16:33). Anyone who desires to live godly will face conflicts without and within.

11. a. How did David describe his feelings in Psalm 42 (verses 3,5,9-10)?

_____

b. What afflictions was David experiencing (verses 2-4,9-10)?

_____

c. How did David respond to his feelings?

_____

12. a. What afflictions did Job suffer (Job 1:14-19, 2:7)?

_____

b. Describe each of Job's responses.

Job 1:20-22 _____

Job 2:7-10 _____

Job 6:8-10, 7:17-21 _____
_____
_____

Job 42:1-6 _____
_____
_____

13. a. List five of Paul's afflictions recorded in 2 Corinthians 11:22-33.

_____
_____
_____
_____

b. Discuss Paul's responses to suffering in 2 Corinthians 12:9-10 and Philippians 4:11-13.

_____
_____
_____
_____
_____

14. a. Describe an affliction you or a friend have experienced recently, and how you have felt and acted because of it.

___

___

___

___

___

___

b. How should you respond to such an experience?

___

___

One final cause of discouragement besides fear, failure, sin, and affliction is a lack of assurance.

LACK OF ASSURANCE

At times when I am counseling someone, he will say, "I'm really discouraged. I pray, but it seems as though God is no longer listening. I'm beginning to question whether or not He is still interested in my welfare. My mind tells me that He loves me, but my feelings are totally numb." When people look at the wars and violence surrounding them, or man's inhumanity to his fellows, they may shake their heads and wonder, "How can God exist and allow these attrocities to continue?"

The Psalmist was troubled that the wicked seemed to enjoy life while the godly experienced all types of problems.

15. How did the Psalmist's discouragement affect him (Psalm 73:2-3,13,16,21-22)?

___

___

___

___

___

16. a. Have you ever experienced anything similar to what the Psalmist described? Explain.

_____
_____
_____
_____
_____

b. How did you deal with the problem?

_____
_____
_____
_____
_____

c. How did the Psalmist handle his problem? What did he learn (Psalm 73:17-20,23-28)?

_____
_____
_____
_____
_____
_____

If you are feeling discouraged, recognize that many of the saints have had to fight the same battle. Sometimes they have won, and sometimes they have known defeat.

In the next chapter you will learn how to win the battle of discouragement. But before you turn to that lesson, evaluate where you are right now.

YOUR RESPONSE
17. Which cause of discouragement most plagues you? Why?

_____

_____

_____

_____

18. How do you currently mean to deal with this problem?

_____

_____

_____

_____

19. Commit yourself this week to deepen your relationship with God by memorizing and repeating at least three of the following affirmations:

> "The one who is in you is greater than the one who is in the world" (1 John 4:4).

> "And my God will meet all your needs according to his glorious riches in Christ Jesus" (Philippians 4:19).

> "I know that you can do all things; no plan of yours can be thwarted. You asked, 'Who is this that obscures my counsel without knowledge?' Surely I spoke of things I did not understand, things too wonderful for me to know" (Job 42:2-3).

> "'For my thoughts are not your thoughts, neither are your ways my ways,' declares the Lord. 'As the heavens are higher than the earth, so are my ways higher than your ways and my thoughts than your thoughts'" (Isaiah 55:8-9).

> "Why are you downcast, O my soul? Why so disturbed within me? Put your hope in God, for I will yet praise him, my Savior and my God" (Psalm 42:5).

Now you are ready to proceed to the next chapter, where you will learn specific ways in which to win against discouragement.

CHAPTER FOUR
THE BATTLE OF DISCOURAGEMENT—ITS CURE

In the last chapter you learned that discouragement may be caused by fear, failure, sin, affliction, and lack of assurance. Although this list of possible causes could be extended, we must now turn from asking "why do I feel discouraged?" to "how can I deal with my discouragement?"

Discouragement is like the common cold: it is contagious, limits your effectiveness, and is difficult to prevent permanently. Even Paul, known for his constant rejoicing, became discouraged at times. He testified to this problem when he wrote, "We do not want you to be uninformed, brothers, about the hardships we suffered in the province of Asia. We were under great pressure, far beyond our ability to endure, so that we despaired even of life" (2 Corinthians 1:8).

There is one other similarity between discouragement and the common cold—neither has an easy cure. You do not cure a cold, you weather it. Likewise, discouragement has no once-for-all cure, but you can cope successfully with it, gaining victory in each battle. I found the following methods helpful in my own battle against discouragement. Focus first on your perspective toward life.

EVALUATE YOUR PERSPECTIVE TOWARD LIFE

The Scriptures reveal how a man's attitude determines his behavior, saying, "for as he thinks within himself, so he is" (Proverbs 23:7 NASB). If he thinks that the whole world is against him, he will act defensively. On the other hand, if he thinks that he has the world by the tail, he will act assertively. If he believes deep down that God can really be trusted to meet his needs, then he will make different choices than if he believes he must look out for himself.

Remembering this premise, consider how basing your perspective on truth can move you from discouragement into hope.

THINK MORE ABOUT WHAT GOD CAN DO THAN ABOUT WHAT YOU CANNOT DO

Ponder some things you have wanted to do but have been afraid they were beyond your reach. What has happened? If you are like most people, you probably have not tried. Or you have made a little effort but soon grew discouraged and gave up.

Remember from the last chapter when God told the Israelites to enter the promised land. They sent spies into the land, saw the giants living there, and concluded, "We can't attack those people; they are stronger than we are. . . . We seemed like grasshoppers in our own eyes, and we looked the same to them" (Numbers 13:31,33).

The spies imagined the power of the land's inhabitants, compared themselves in light of that perception, and so were discouraged. They neglected to look at God's power. Two of the spies tried to draw their attention to what God could do for them. They pleaded, "'If the Lord is pleased with us, he will lead us into that land, a land flowing with milk and honey, and will give it to us. Only do not rebel against the Lord. And do not be afraid of the people of the land, because we will swallow them up. Their protection is gone, but the Lord is with us. Do not be afraid of them'" (Numbers 14:8-9). But the Israelites would not listen because of fear.

1. Read John 15:1-5. What resource does Jesus offer the believer to accomplish great works (verses 4-5)? (What does it mean to "remain" or "abide" in Jesus? See also Philippians 2:12-13.)

   _____
   _____
   _____

2. Why does God want you to be fruitful in the things you do (John 15:8)?

3. a. Does God stop loving you if you fail at the tasks He sets before you (Ephesians 2:8-10)? Why, or why not?

   b. What then should be your motive for doing good?

4. How can you find out what works to attempt?

5. After applying these methods, list two projects you could undertake which would honor God.

   a. _____

   b. _____

6. Explain God's promise to you if you do not give up (Galatians 6:9).

A second perspective to help you deal with discouragement is to review what God has already done for you.

REVIEW WHAT GOD HAS ALREADY DONE FOR YOU

Sometimes we lose our bearings because we do not have a sense of history. It is difficult to know where you should go if you do not know where you have been. Furthermore, spiritual development is not just the result of precept upon precept, but also experience upon experience as you observe the faithfulness of God. Today I can trust God for accomplishments which I would have felt impossible a few years ago because I have witnessed His faithfulness over the years. As I review God's past provisions, I develop greater faith for the future.

7. What did Joshua have his people do to remember God's faithfulness (Joshua 4:18-24)?

   _____

   _____

   _____

8. How can you make reminders for yourself of God's provision?

   _____

   _____

   _____

   _____

   _____

Besides looking to God's ability and remembering His past faithfulness to you, you can also remember that God is still in control.

REMEMBER THAT GOD IS STILL IN CONTROL

Circumstances have a way of clouding our thinking. When pressures mount and everything seems to be falling apart around us, it is difficult to believe that God is still in control.

9. To steady yourself in those moments, look up the following three verses, write them out in the spaces

below, and then commit them to memory.

Job 42:2 _____

_____

_____

Jeremiah 29:11 _____

_____

_____

_____

Daniel 4:35 _____

_____

_____

_____

God is in control of life's events. This does not mean that He agrees with everything that happens, nor that He causes all things to occur. But it does mean that nothing can be done apart from what He permits. You may wonder why He permits certain events to take place; the answer to this question unfolds the fourth perspective you must adopt to vanquish discouragement.

RECOGNIZE THE PURPOSES OF PROBLEMS
No one enjoys problems. But they are necessary, like fertilizer—sometimes overpowering to the senses, but essential for productivity.

10. Consult the following Scripture passages, and explain the purposes of hardship in each case.

   Genesis 37:2,18,27; 45:4-11 _____

   _____

   _____

   Deuteronomy 8:2,16 _____

   _____

   _____

Romans 5:3-4 _____
_____
_____

James 1:2-4 _____
_____

1 Peter 1:6-7 _____
_____

Like the dark clouds of a storm, problems can inspire gloom and despair. Yet when the storm is past, all appears refreshed; you breathe deeply, filling your lungs with the crisp, clean air. Even so, when times of testing overwhelm you, remember that God not only is using those problems for your benefit, but will also bring you through them triumphantly. Expect the success which He alone can create.

EXPECT GOD TO GIVE YOU SUCCESS
At times I feel I am up to my armpits with alligators. Everything seems to be snapping around me, with no escape in sight. Discouragement hovers. When I focus on the hopelessness of the situation, discouragement engulfs me. But when I remind myself that God is responsible for my success and alone can bring it to pass, then discouragement flees and peace fills my heart.

11. Galatians 6:9 promises eternal reward for "doing good" if we fulfill two related conditions. What are they?

_____
_____

12. From 1 Corinthians 3:6, explain your responsibility and God's responsibility in your works of service.

_____
_____
_____
_____

How is your perspective? Do you spend most of your time looking at your weakness or God's strength? Do you review what God has already done for you? Do you really believe that He is in control, or that He has your best interest in mind when He allows problems to confront you? Are you expecting Him to give success in tasks which please Him, and abandoning those which do not?

These perspectives are foreign to many people because <u>the world teaches that we can rely only on ourselves</u>. Believing that God either cannot act, does not care, loves only those who succeed, or helps only those who help themselves, many people grow discouraged. To shake off these false beliefs, enlist the aid of other Christians.

DEVELOP A SUPPORT SYSTEM

People need people. That is what the church is all about—it is God's support system for the individual and the family. However, it does not always function that way.

13. From the passages below, explain how Paul reminded the churches of their responsibility, challenging believers to support one another within the Body of Christ.

    Romans 12:10 _____

    _____

    Romans 14:1 _____

    _____

    Romans 15:5-6 _____

    _____

    1 Thessalonians 4:13-18 _____

    _____

    _____

    1 Thessalonians 5:6-11 _____

    _____

14. Describe how you might begin to apply this counsel in your church. Whose help can you get?

_____
_____
_____
_____
_____
_____
_____
_____

Do support systems actually help a person's well-being? In his book *Stress and the Bottom Line*, stress management specialist Dr. E.M. Gherman writes, "People who are functioning members of their community who are 'socially healthy' also tend to have a higher degree of psychological health and physical well-being. Those people who have developed a source of social support, who have close friendships, strong family ties, and warm relationships with neighbors and fellow workers, generally deal more effectively with stressful events than those who are socially isolated."[1]

Thirdly, you can deal discouragement a tremendous blow by adding another weapon—the gift of yourself to others.

GIVE YOURSELF TO OTHERS

If you think of those times when you are most discouraged, you will probably find it is when you are burning up your energy thinking about yourself: "Why doesn't anything seem to go my way?" "Why did this have to happen to me?" "What's in it for me?"

Try another approach at such times. Give yourself to others. Get involved in others' lives, and you will soon find yourself thanking God that your problems are not that bad after all.

15. How did Jesus set examples of this attitude?

    Matthew 4:23-24 _____
_____

Matthew 20:25-28

16. a. Restate in your own words how Jesus expressed this principle in Luke 9:24.

b. Why is this strange truth true? Think about your most deepfelt needs and how Scripture says they can be met. (See Matthew 6:33; Romans 8:35,39; Ephesians 2:10; Philippians 4:19.)

A young missionary once put this truth into practice by literally giving his life that the Auca Indians might hear about Jesus. He said, "He is no fool who gives what he cannot keep to gain what he cannot lose."[2]

One final weapon against discouragement is worthwhile goals.

SET WORTHWHILE GOALS

Several years ago we brought a consultant into our church to help us think through where we had been and where we were going. After spending about nine grueling months evaluating, reorganizing, and establishing goals, I was running low on energy. We had met many setbacks in pursuing our goals. Two days after returning from a vacation I was in a church board meeting, unable to answer the board's questions about some areas of ministry. I was embarrassingly unprepared and felt like a bumbling idiot. I left the meeting at an all-time emotional low, convinced that all of the past nine months' work had been in vain.

Later in the week, my friend Bobb Biehl of Masterplanning Associates met with me. After I poured out my woes to him, he asked me to look over my planning arrow (a system he designed for setting goals and achieving objectives) again, and to tell how many of my goals had been achieved during the past nine months. To my delight, I could reply that about eighty-five percent had already been accomplished. What an encouragement that was for a guy who was dragging through a slough of despondency! The same can happen to you when you set written goals. They not only keep you on course, but also provide a sense of accomplishment.

17. Name the goal-setters in the following passages, and describe their goals.

   1 Chronicles 28:2,5-6 _____

   _____

   Nehemiah 1:1, 2:17 _____

   _____

   Luke 19:10 _____

   _____

   Romans 1:5 _____

   _____

   Romans 8:28-29 _____

   _____

18. What practices are crucial when you set goals, and why?

   Proverbs 15:22 _____

   _____

   _____

   _____

Proverbs 16:2-3 (What does it meant to "Commit to the Lord whatever you do"?)

_____

James 4:13-17 _____

19. List three specific goals that you would like to reach within the next six months. (Consider such areas as your family, finances, spiritual life, job, physical exercise, personal growth, etc. Do not even think of leaving God out of such decisions.)

a. _____

b. _____

c. _____

20. How have the three practices of question 18 affected (and not affected) how you set these three goals? How will they affect how you will now approach these goals?

_____

When discouragement knocks at your door, you do not have to invite it in. You now have four weapons at your disposal for your battle against discouragement. You can: 1) evaluate your perspective toward life; 2) develop or join a support system; 3) give yourself to others; and 4) establish worthwhile goals.

These weapons are helpful only to the point that you use them. Take hold then of the opportunities which are before you, and in the thick of battle, remember these words, "The Lord himself goes before you and will be with you; he will never leave you nor forsake you. Do not be afraid; do not be discouraged" (Deuteronomy 31:8).

1. Gherman, E.M. *Stress and the Bottom Line: A Guide to Personal Well-Being and Corporate Health* (New York: American Management Association, Inc., 1981), page 265.
2. Elisabeth Elliot, *Shadow of the Almighty* (San Francisco: Harper and Row, 1956), page 15.

CHAPTER FIVE
THE BATTLE OF COVETOUSNESS

The political opportunist driven to conquer more territory, the gambler under the spell of promised instant wealth, and the man enslaved to wallow in sexual promiscuity all have one characteristic in common—covetousness. Scripture uses several words to convey the concept of covetousness. These include *epithumeo*, "to desire, long for" (used in both a good and a bad sense); *orego*, "to strive for, reach after" (1 Timothy 6:10); *pleonexia*, "greediness, covetousness, a desire to have more" (1 Thessalonians 2:5); and *philarguros*, "a money lover" (Luke 16:14, 2 Timothy 3:2).

From these words we can define covetousness as "an unsatisfied desire which craves for more without regard to God's will." To love a person within the guidelines of Scripture is proper, but love turns to lust when we violate God's standards by committing immorality. We are saying in essence, "I know that it's wrong, but I must fulfill this desire whether God approves or not."

This chapter will help you see greediness for what it really is—an uncontrolled desire. You will also learn how to fight the battle of greed successfully.

EXAMPLES OF GREED

OLD TESTAMENT EXAMPLES
  1. a. Read Numbers 11:4-9. What did the people of Israel crave (verse 4)?

---

b. How did what God provided for them differ from what they desired (verses 7-9)?

_____
_____
_____

c. Describe their attitude toward God's provision and the values behind it (verses 5-6). How did the people misunderstand their needs?

_____
_____
_____
_____

2. How do you sometimes show your ingratitude for the way God has provided for you?

_____
_____
_____
_____

The book of Joshua records another instance of greediness. The people had just won an unprecedented victory over the city of Jericho. Every Israelite was overwhelmed by the way God had delivered the city into their hands. But in the midst of this triumph, a lone Israelite was losing a personal battle against greed. He violated the Lord's command to destroy as unclean all the possessions of pagan Jericho.

3. Read Joshua 7:1-5,20-26. Write the action verbs which describe Achan's battle and defeat (verse 21). (The New International Version uses four action verbs. Your translation may differ.)

   a. _____
   b. _____

c. _____

d. _____

4. What were the results of this man's defeat?

   Joshua 7:1-5 _____
   _____

   Joshua 7:22-26 _____
   _____

NEW TESTAMENT EXAMPLES

5. Study each of the following passages. For each, record *who* lost to greed, *how* they showed greed, and *what beliefs* (about God, their needs, etc.) lay behind their greed.

   Matthew 5:27-28 _____
   _____
   _____
   _____

   Luke 12:13-20 _____
   _____
   _____
   _____
   _____
   _____
   _____

   Acts 5:1-11 _____
   _____
   _____
   _____
   _____

Acts 8:14-24 _____

_____
_____
_____
_____

Desire in itself is neither good nor bad. But desire becomes lust when one of the following conditions is met: 1) when your desire exploits others, uses them, or takes advantage of them; 2) when your desire controls you; 3) when you must go against God's will to fulfill it; or 4) when it makes you impatient so that you try to satisfy it outside of God's timing or priorities.

Another way to better understand greed is to look at some of its opposites.

OPPOSITES OF GREED

6. a. What word recurs in Philippians 4:11, 1 Timothy 6:6, and Hebrews 13:5?

_____

b. In each case, what reason is given for this attitude?

Philippians 4:13 _____

_____

1 Timothy 6:7,9 _____

_____

Hebrews 13:5 _____

_____

7. a. How did Paul encourage the Corinthians to deal with the potential problem of covetousness (2 Corinthians 8:3-5, 9:5-7)?

_____
_____
_____

b. Why would this method work?

8. How would you distinguish between love and lust? (Consider 1 Corinthians 13:4).

9. a. Read Genesis 13:8-13, 14:17-24. Who was the greedy of these two men, and how did he show his greed?

b. How did the other man show that he was not greedy?

Now that you have observed some examples of greed and its opposite, consider the sources of greed. The lust which every believer experiences at times emerges from both within and without.

THE SOURCES OF GREED
10. Explain the source of greed which each of the following passages discusses. How does each source produce greed in us?

Genesis 3:1-6 _____
_____
_____

James 1:14-15 _____
_____
_____

1 John 2:16 _____
_____
_____

You should be able to see now why the battles of covetousness, greed, and lust are such struggles. You are being attacked from three sides. However, in spite of greed's powerful attraction, you do not have to fall victim to its enticement. You can win the battle. The Scriptures offer at least six strategies for dealing with greed—four preventive and two corrective.

THE STRATEGIES TO WIN OVER GREED

THE PREVENTIVE APPROACH
Many Christians live like the farmer who closed the barn door after the horse got out. He could have prevented the loss by securing the door while the horse was still inside the barn. Likewise, believers often spend too much time confessing failure and too little preventing it.

11. a. How did Jesus teach an inquirer to prevent greed in Luke 12:15?
_____

b. Name some specific way by which you could fulfill that command.
_____
_____

12. a. What attitudes does Jesus want us to cultivate to prevent covetousness and encourage contentment?

    Luke 12:23 _____

    Luke 12:24,27-28 _____

    Luke 12:25-26 _____

    Luke 12:31-32 _____

    b. How can you acquire these attitudes?

    _____
    _____
    _____
    _____

13. a. Review question 7. Why did Jesus recommend the action of Luke 12:33?

    _____
    _____
    _____

    b. How does this counsel apply to you?

    _____
    _____
    _____
    _____
    _____
    _____

14. a. Explain the meaning of Paul's instruction in Galatians 5:16.

_____
_____
_____

b. How can you be certain that you are following this command?

_____
_____
_____
_____

THE CORRECTIVE APPROACH

The Scriptures also provide counsel as to what you should do when a compromising situation is causing your passions to stir.

15. a. What does Paul advise in 2 Timothy 2:22?

_____
_____

b. Describe how Joseph used this strategy (Genesis 39:7-12).

_____
_____
_____
_____

16. What other strategy against greed does Paul offer (Colossians 3:5)?

_____

One way of putting something to death is to starve or neglect it. We fan the flames of passion and greed when we continually feed our minds with material that excites the desire to possess. But if we refrain from feeding on what stirs our passions and instead center on thoughts of God and His purposes and acts, we will increasingly gain victory.

17. Think of the greed which most tempts you. How can you put it to death?

_____
_____
_____
_____
_____

RESPONDING TO TRUTH

Truth without application becomes as stagnant as a cesspool. But as you apply these principles to your life, you will begin to experience a well of pure water flowing from within you and refreshing every area of your life. So respond to this chapter by answering these final questions, and then take action!

18. What is the most significant fact that you learned from this chapter?

_____
_____
_____

19. What specific action will you take in order to win the battle of covetousness?

_____
_____
_____
_____
_____
_____

CHAPTER SIX
THE BATTLE OF PHYSICAL IMPAIRMENT

Our bodies and our health are very important to us. Americans spend billions annually for cosmetics alone. We dump even more millions into the coffers of health clubs and health food stores. Most Americans are on diets. That is not all bad, since one-quarter of all women ages 20 to 74 weigh at least twenty percent more than the optimal weight for their height. About fourteen percent of men in the same age group are substantially overweight, and almost half of all American adults believe they have a weight problem.

Dr. James Dobson speaks about the emphasis we place on beauty when he writes, "Without question, the most highly valued personal attribute in our culture (and in most others) is physical attractiveness."[1] So what happens when one's health, youth, or physical attractiveness is removed? And how does the person who has never had either physical attractiveness nor good health react to a society that worships both? The effects are often devastating and may include feelings of inferiority, depression, anger at God, self-pity, and so forth.

Does the devil play a part in our health and physical handicaps? The Bible indicates that he does. He has the power to afflict people physically, but only within God's permissive will.

Having made that statement, I am not implying that every physical defect or every handicap is caused by satanic attack. The Lord has not seen fit to reveal why He allows certain individuals to suffer the loss of a limb, or experience paralysis, or live for years with poor health. Certainly we are all vulnerable to the effects of the world's long corruption. But the Scriptures do uncover that in some cases Satan is directly aggravating a problem, and in probably all cases he attempts to discourage and defeat those who experience physical problems.

Therefore, take a look at two of God's servants and learn about their problems, how they coped with them, and what they learned about their physical afflictions.

THE PROBLEMS

JOB
In Chapter Three you caught a glimpse of Job. Now take a closer look, focusing on his physical problems.

1. a. What kind of man was Job (Job 1:1)?

    _____

    b. What problems did he face before he experienced health problems (Job 1:13-19)?

    _____

    _____

    _____

    c. Describe Job's health problem (Job 2:7).

    _____

    _____

PAUL
2. a. How did Paul describe his handicap in 2 Corinthians 12:7?

    _____

    b. What caused his problem?

    _____

    c. Was it temporary or permanent (2 Corinthians 12:8-9)?

    _____

Remember that both Job and Paul were godly men. God was not punishing them for some gross sin. But both of them became objects of the enemy's scheme to bring them to ruin. Satan wanted both men to curse God for allowing their physical problems to develop.

The stresses of life are due less to the problems and pressures that we face than to the way we respond to them. Some people never handle their problems well, while others sail through them beautifully. Consider how these two men dealt with their handicaps.

THE COPING METHOD

JOB

3. a. How did Job respond to his physical problem (Job 2:9-10)?

   _____

   _____

   b. How did he sometimes feel (Job 3:1,11,20-26)?

   _____

   _____

   _____

Few people ever experience a quick victory over their physical afflictions. Most of the time they are up one day and down the next. They accept it as part of God's plan one day, but may want to throw in the towel the next day. Like any other problem in life, coping is a learned process and takes time. It will usually include many victories and defeats.

4. What gave Job comfort through his long trial?

   Job 6:10 _____

   Job 10:12 _____

   Job 10:13-14 _____

   Job 23:12 _____

Job was really hurting during his affliction. After all, he not only had poor health, but also had lost his wealth and his children. Furthermore, he did not have the advantage of three thousand years of biblical truth to which he could turn. In light of this, it is amazing how well he did cope. Now see how Paul dealt with his problem.

PAUL

5. a. How did Paul try to gain healing (2 Corinthians 12:8)?

_____

b. When that did not work, what was Paul's alternate approach (2 Corinthians 12:9-10)?

_____

_____

_____

It is significant that a man who was able on occasion to heal others was not able to heal himself. In my book *Discover Your Spiritual Gift and Use It* I list three reasons why God may not bring healing, even though we believe that He can and are walking closely with Him.

What about faith? Can't we always expect God to heal if we really have faith? No, not necessarily.

1. God may withhold healing as a *discipline because of sin*. In Corinth there was a case of incest in the church. A man was living immorally with his stepmother. Paul warned, "I have decided to deliver such a one to Satan for the destruction of his flesh, that his spirit may be saved in the day of the Lord Jesus" (1 Corinthians 5:5). Apparently this man was stricken with an illness as a direct discipline for sin. Later, however, he did repent and Paul asked the church to restore him to fellowship (2 Corinthians 2:6-11).
. . .

2. However, personal sin isn't the only reason for God's withholding the healing of the body. He may withhold healing for our *personal growth*. For instance, illness may add *humility* to our character (2 Corinthians 12:7-9).

Paul had a lot to boast about. He was well educated, he possessed an excellent Jewish religious heritage. He was zealous for God. He had seen the resurrected Christ, and then he had the privilege of seeing what heaven was like. What he saw was so marvelous he wasn't permitted to share his experience with others (2 Corinthians 12:4).

Paul could have gotten a 'big head' because of these great experiences. He might have begun thinking that God favored him above all others. So he tells us that God permitted Satan to afflict him physically. God would not heal him. . . .

Illness may add *empathy* to our character. Paul teaches us that affliction prepares us for service. 'Blessed be the God and Father of our Lord Jesus Christ, the Father of mercies and God of all comfort; who comforts us in all our affliction *so that we may be able to comfort* those who are in any affliction with the comfort with which we ourselves are comforted by God' (2 Corinthians 1:3-4). It isn't surprising that those who have tasted long illness desire to help others going through an illness. They are capable of 'feeling' with those who are sick.

3. Another possible reason why God doesn't always heal immediately, or at times not at all, is that he may receive greater glory in a person's sickness than in his recovery. Illness may *add to God's glory.*

When Jesus and his disciples had gone out of the temple one day, they spotted a man who was blind from birth. "And His disciples asked Him, saying, 'Rabbi, who sinned, this man or his parents, that he should be born blind?' Jesus answered, 'It was neither that this man sinned, nor his parents; but it was in order that the works of God might be displayed in him.'" (John 9:2-3). God didn't want this man healed early in life. He had his own timetable. And it wasn't until that very day that God was prepared to heal him.

Emily Gardiner Neal was an agnostic reporter who determined to expose the myth of healing. But in the process of her research she found Christ. She writes, "We are often led astray by the false assumption that God can be glorified only by a witness of physical healing. The truth is that some of the most effective Christian witnesses I know are those who are lying flat on their backs expectantly awaiting their healing by God's grace and at the same time are offering their suffering to be used for His glory."

It's important to remember that in one situation God is glorified by healing. In another he is glorified by withholding healing.

God cannot be programmed. He cannot be confined to one purpose or one method. He is an unlimited God who is carrying out his purposes in our lives....[2]

6. In Romans 8:28 Paul wrote that "in all things God works for the good of those who love Him." If God uses an evil such as suffering to produce good, is it then not evil? (How does *permitting* an event differ from *causing* it?)

_____
_____
_____
_____

Whether God delivers us from our handicap or not, He does want us to learn something about Himself and about ourselves. Investigate the lessons which Job and Paul learned.

LESSONS

JOB

7. What did Job learn through his temporary handicap?

Job 42:1-3 _____

_____

Job 42:4 _____

_____

Job 42:5-6 _____

_____

8. How did God provide for Job (Job 42:10-17)?

_____
_____
_____
_____

9. Do you think these provisions nullified for Job his previous sufferings and the deaths of his first family? Why?

_____
_____
_____
_____

10. How do you think his change in fortunes affected Job's attitude toward God? Why?

_____
_____
_____
_____

PAUL

11. What did Paul learn through his permanent handicap concerning its purpose (2 Corinthians 12:7)?

_____
_____

12. What did he learn about God's grace (2 Corinthians 12:9-10)?

_____
_____
_____

You have seen that both Job and Paul were afflicted with physical problems. One was temporary; the other was permanent. Neither man welcomed the problem. Both asked God to deliver them from their afflictions. God delivered Job but allowed Paul to remain handicapped with his thorn in the flesh. But before Job's relief of physical distress and Paul's complete victory over a permanent handicap, both men came to accept their problems as part of God's plan for their lives.

Dr. Elizabeth Kubler-Ross, author of *Death and Dying*, has observed five stages that a terminally ill patient goes through. I believe the physically handicapped and those who have poor health experience the same stages.

1. SHOCK AND DENIAL—"No, not me."
2. ANGER— "Why me?"
3. BARGAINING WITH GOD—"Yes me, but . . ." "If you deliver me, I will . . ."
4. DEPRESSION—"I have nothing to look forward to."
5. ACCEPTANCE—"Lord, I don't know why, but I pray for your strength to see me through this. Teach me what I need to know. Use this affliction for your honor."

You may be permanently crippled or experiencing a temporary setback because of an accident or illness. Whether this problem is the direct result of satanic affliction is not important. What is essential is that you not allow the enemy to gain victory over you while you are suffering. God wants to use you for His beautiful plan as you are. He will if you give Him your permission.

Consider how the Lord has used Joni Eareckson Tada. Without her affliction, Joni would probably be an attractive housewife with children running around the house. Most people would consider that an ideal, but Joni would never have made the impact on others that she has. It is one thing for a healthy person to talk about God's sufficiency in trials, but quite another when a pretty girl rejoices in the Lord as she sits in a wheelchair as a quadriplegic.

Your battle may be a physical problem. But you do not have to be defeated. You can win the war by letting God use your circumstances.

1. James Dobson, *Hide or Seek* (Old Tappan, New Jersey: Fleming H. Revell, 1979), page 15.
2. Rick Yohn, *Discover Your Spiritual Gift and Use It* (Wheaton, Illinois: Tyndale House Publishers, 1982), pages 30-32.

CHAPTER SEVEN
THE BATTLE OF SELFISHNESS

1. a. For whose sake should we live, and how (2 Corinthians 4:5,8-11,15)?

   _____

   _____

   _____

   b. Why (2 Corinthians 4:6, 5:14-15)?

   _____

   _____

   _____

Have you ever experienced the humiliation of sliding from the height of being a hero to the depth of being a goat, all in one week? A young business executive identifies with the problem as he enters the office one morning and is congratulated by his boss for winning a profitable contract with a large company the night before. He enjoys the accolades other senior executives heap upon him, and the envy of his peers as well.

Reveling in his hero status, he decides to tackle a difficult but lucrative contract with another potential client. As he wines and dines the prospect, however, he discovers that he will have to make some concessions to get the customer's business. Although he does not have the authority to make such concessions, he promises his client that he will have no difficulty living up to the agreement. The contract is signed, and the young executive rushes back to the office to inform his boss of what he has achieved. But instead of the praise he expected, the young man receives a torrent of verbal abuse from a senior executive who has just come apart at the seams. The boss accuses his subordinate of not having the company's interest at heart, of making concessions to serve his own interests. The boss explains how his underhanded decision will cost the company thousands of dollars. A hero? No longer. Instead he feels the shame that often accompanies selfish interest and selfish ambition.

The Gospels report two incidents when the battle of selfishness was fought and lost. The key figure in the one was Peter, who changed from hero to goat in one day. In the other case, the selfish one was Judas Iscariot. The first account highlights self-interest, while the second uncovers selfish ambition. We will begin this lesson by evaluating Peter's battle with selfish interest.

PETER AND HIS SELF-INTEREST (MATTHEW 16:21-26)

What is self-interest? It is not necessarily synonymous with personal interest. You may be interested in playing tennis, listening to good music, or traveling to a foreign country. These may be valid personal interests which can be fulfilled without hurting anyone. But *self-interest* describes "that driving desire which consumes thought, time, energy, and possibly money spent on oneself at the expense of God and others."[1]

Self-interest always conflicts with God's interest. This is why Jesus so strongly opposed Peter's comments. Consider the dialogue between Jesus and Peter in Matthew's Gospel.

Earlier that day Peter had been a hero. When Jesus had asked His profound question, "Who do you say I am?" Peter had wisely replied, "You are the Christ, the Son of the living God" (Matthew 16:15-16). Although the other disciples may have come to the same conclusion, it was Peter who verbalized it. Thus, he had deserved Jesus' commendation, "Blessed are you, Simon son of Jonah, for this was not revealed to you by man, but by my Father in heaven" (Matthew 16:17).

But soon after his great confession, Peter put his foot

in his mouth. As Jesus began to reveal to His disciples the meaning of Christhood, the necessity of His suffering and death, Peter stepped in where angels fear to tread. Still proud of his previous insight, Peter took the Lord aside and began to rebuke Him, chiding, "Never, Lord! . . . This shall never happen to You" (Matthew 16:22).

What was Peter really saying? In what way was he entrapped in his own self-interest?

GOD'S PLAN

2. a. Read Matthew 26:67-68 and 27:26-31,38-44,46,50. Describe what God had planned for His Christ to experience.

b. How was Jesus supposed to respond (1 Peter 2:23)?

3. What do you think was Peter's plan for the Christ (Zechariah 9:9-13; Matthew 21:5,9; 26:51)?

4. If Peter had convinced Jesus to follow his plan, what would you have lost? Explain in your own words what each of the following verses teaches about God's purpose in Christ's suffering.

2 Corinthians 5:21

73

Hebrews 2:18 _____

_____

Hebrews 4:15-16 _____

_____

_____

Hebrews 10:4,11-12 _____

_____

_____

_____

5. Why was Peter's plan selfish?

_____

_____

_____

_____

A BETTER IDEA

Can you identify with Peter at this point? I certainly can. It is fallen human nature to attempt to improve upon God's plan. In prayer we inform God not only what we want Him to do, but also how to fulfill our request. When the Lord seems not to be playing by our rules or fitting into our time schedule, we become confused or discouraged, feeling that He has rejected us.

6. Read James 4:13-17. Below, describe the sinful attitude and why it is sinful, and the godly attitude and why it is godly.

sinful _____

_____

_____

godly _____

_____

_____

How often have you told the Lord or yourself, "I'll never do this or be that"? Many years ago, when I was a Christian education director, I vowed, "I'll never be a preacher." My wife vowed within herself, "I'll never move to California." Since then we have both decided to stop stating what we will never be or do, because today I am a preacher and we lived in California for thirteen years.

7. How do people attempt to improve on God's ideas? The two columns below contrast God's original idea with what man thinks is his better idea. Explain God's idea from each Scripture reference.

GOD'S ORIGINAL IDEAS	MAN'S "BETTER" IDEAS
Matthew 19:3-9 _____	Stay married until you can't get along with one another.
Hebrews 13:4 _____	Sexual intimacy is fine whenever you desire and with whomever you desire.
Ephesians 5:25 _____	A husband may use his wife as he pleases since she is his. A husband may give his love to another woman if he find his wife unlovable.
Ephesians 5:22 _____	A wife is her own person, subject to no one.

GOD'S ORIGINAL IDEAS	MAN'S "BETTER" IDEAS
Genesis 4:1-2, Jeremiah 1:5 _____	It is alright to abort a conceived baby if you do not want it.
Deuteronomy 8:18 _____ 1 Timothy 6:17-19 _____	Money is a commodity you may spend however you desire. You earn it.
Acts 2:38, 4:12 _____ John 1:12 _____	God will accept you if you are ethical and sincere in whatever religion you follow.

Jesus rebuked Peter by saying, "Out of my sight, Satan! You are a stumbling block to me; you do not have in mind the things of God, but the things of men" (Matthew 16:23).

8. a. Why do you think Jesus addressed Peter as Satan?

_____
_____
_____

b. How was Peter a stumbling block to Jesus?

_____
_____
_____

9. How may we be stumbling blocks to others when we have our own interests at heart? Give an example from your life.

_____
_____
_____
_____
_____

How should you make decisions so as not to become a stumbling block to others? What questions could you ask that would help reduce self-interest in your decisions? Here is a list of questions to use as a guide when you are making decisions:

    a. Does it violate any biblical principle?
    b. Will it fill a true need?
    c. Will it cause me to depend upon God?
    d. Is it the best way to accomplish God's purpose?
    e. Is it the right time?
    f. Are my motives pure?
    g. Will it ultimately honor God?

10. Choose a decision with which you are currently faced. Prayerfully apply these seven questions to it.

a. _____

b. _____

c. _____

d. _____

e. _____

f. _____

g. _____

Having looked at Peter and his self-interest, consider Judas Iscariot and his selfish ambition.

JUDAS ISCARIOT AND HIS SELFISH AMBITION (MATTHEW 26:14-16, 27:3-5, JOHN 12:1-8, 13:18-30)

Ambition can be either good or bad. In a good sense, it is a strong desire to succeed, to achieve, to accomplish God's purpose. Paul encourages the Thessalonian believers, "Make it your ambition to lead a quiet life, to mind your own business and to work with your hands, just as we told you, so that your daily life may win the respect of outsiders and so that you will not be dependent on anybody" (1 Thessalonians 4:11-12).

But in a bad sense, ambition is a compulsive desire to succeed at the expense of others. James writes, "But if you harbor bitter envy and selfish ambition in your hearts, do not boast about it or deny the truth. . . . For where you have envy and selfish ambition, there you find disorder and every evil practice" (James 3:14,16).

Judas was so controlled by selfish ambition that he was willing to betray a close friend in order to succeed. Three facts about Judas' ambition stand out.

JUDAS' SELFISH AMBITION WAS HIDDEN FROM HIS FRIENDS

11. What pretense did Judas use to cover up his selfish ambition (John 12:3-6)?

_____

_____

12. What was his real interest (John 12:6)?

_____

_____

13. a. What influenced Judas to fulfill his selfish ambition (John 13:27)?

_____

b. Why did his ambition make him vulnerable to this influence?

_____

_____

_____

14. Why were his friends so unsuspecting (John 13:28-30)?

_____

_____

15. What are some of the major objects of selfish ambition?

Matthew 6:2,5,16 _____

Luke 16:14 _____

Philippians 1:15-17 _____

1 Peter 5:3 _____

Judas was a master of deception. He had learned how to hide his real intentions. None of his friends suspected him. After all, was not this the disciple who had such a soft heart for the poor? But Jesus was not deceived.

JUDAS' SELFISH AMBITION WAS KNOWN TO JESUS.

16. a. How did Jesus refer to Judas, even before the betrayal (John 6:70-71)?

_____

b. What evidence did Jesus give that he knew Judas' heart (John 13:21-26)?

_____

_____

c. According to Proverbs 16:2, how are we in the same position as Judas?

_____

_____

Most people who are selfishly ambitious have convinced themselves that this is the way to be fulfilled in life. Like all of us, they need to feel that they matter—have an impact, a purpose—but the selfishly ambitious fail to see that only by listening to God can we find our true purposes. Thus, rather than receiving a greater quality of life, those who pursue earthly success lose quality.

Like Peter, Judas had expected Jesus to become an earthly conqueror who could reward his friends with power. But while Peter's love for Jesus triumphed over his disillusionment, Judas changed sides when it seemed he had backed a loser. His goal was to survive and to seek power through others later.

JUDAS' SELFISH AMBITION RESULTED IN PERSONAL TRAGEDY (MATTHEW 27:3-5).

17. What was Judas' first response when he achieved his survival by betraying Jesus (Matthew 27:3-4)?

_____

_____

_____

18. a. How did Judas respond when he discovered at last that his route to personal worth was false (Matthew 27:5)?

    b. What else could a person do when he makes such a discovery (Luke 15:21)?

19. How does James describe the result of selfish ambition (James 3:16)?

20. Discuss a situation in which you have seen the results of selfish ambition.

People are not things to be manipulated for our own purposes; they are God's creatures in need of love and placed on this planet to help fulfill His masterplan.

As a child of God, each of us is responsible to work toward fitting into God's plan. As you discover His unique plan for you, there will be no need to compete or be jealous about what He has planned for someone else. Therefore Paul could write, "Do nothing out of selfish ambition or vain conceit, but in humility consider others better than yourselves. Each of you should look not only to your own interests, but also to the interests of others" (Philippians 2:3-4).

YOUR RESPONSE
21. a. Name someone toward whom you have had twinges of jealousy. (Perhaps a brother, sister, fellow worker, someone at church, etc.) What thoughts and feelings have you had toward that person?

_____
_____
_____
_____
_____
_____

b. What wrong understanding of God's plan have your thoughts shown?

_____
_____
_____
_____

22. Confess your jealousy and begin to pray for God to bless that person. Ask God to show you how to respond encouragingly to that person.

CHAPTER EIGHT
WHAT ARE MY RESOURCES

You have marched through five battlefields in this Bible study, witnessing the victories and defeats of some of God's servants. You have learned strategies which will help you win your own battles. To conclude this study, let us examine the equipment which God has provided to give you consistent victory. The sixth chapter of Ephesians calls it God's panoply (armor).

1. Read Ephesians 6:11-20. What defense system does Paul encourage his readers to use, and what does he say is its purpose (Ephesians 6:13)?

   _____

   _____

In the Greek of verse 11, Paul tells the believer to "put on" the full armor of God, but in verse 13 he says to "take up" the armor. The phrases mean essentially the same thing, except that you must first pick up the armor before you put it on. The entire armor is at your disposal, but it will be effective only as you pick it up and put it on.

2. Why do you believe it is important to use the *full* armor of God?

   _____

   _____

   _____

THE BELT OF TRUTH

The belt of the Roman soldier was six to eight inches wide. It wrapped around the waist, and every other part of the armor was attached to it.

   3. Each of the following verses discusses an aspect of the truth you already possess if you are a Christian. For each, explain *why* Scripture calls it the truth and *how* you can more tightly enwrap yourself in it.

      John 14:6 _____

      _____

      _____

      _____

      _____

      John 15:26, 16:13-14 _____

      _____

      _____

      _____

      _____

The truth is valuable because it helps you know more about your enemy and his devilish schemes. It also provides wisdom for you to understand how to gain victory over him. If you are devoted to discerning and practicing truth, you are less likely to be deceived by his lies. You will know your true status before God despite your enemy's accusations and the true benefits of obeying God despite the devil's temptations.

   4. Explain why each of the following is a result of knowing and conforming to the truth.

      a. It will make you free (John 8:31-36]).

      _____

      _____

      _____

b. By it you will be made holy (John 17:17).

c. It will make the Church and each believer mature and united (Ephesians 4:14-15).

d. It will equip you for good work (2 Timothy 3:16-17).

5. Write out a truth you have come across recently which has in some way changed your attitudes, values, or behavior. Describe how it has changed you.

6. What does Satan do with truth?

   Luke 8:11-12 _____

John 8:44 _____

_____

2 Corinthians 4:3-4 _____

_____

2 Corinthians 11:13-15 _____

_____

7. How do you need currently to resist his efforts?

_____

_____

_____

_____

THE BREASTPLATE OF RIGHTEOUSNESS
The breastplate was divided into two sections protecting the front and the back of the soldier, his heart and his lungs. Righteousness is the standard which God requires from the believer. It includes being right with God and doing what is right.

8. What mistake do many people make about righteous living (Romans 10:3-4)?

_____

_____

_____

9. Where can one discover God's righteousness (Romans 1:17)?

_____

10. How does one receive this righteousness (Romans 4:3, 10:8-10)?

_____

_____

_____

11. Since the believer possesses God's righteousness, why is he told in 1 Timothy 6:11 to pursue righteousness? (Compare 1 John 2:29.)

_____
_____
_____
_____
_____

The devil has a difficult time defeating the believer who not only possesses Christ's righteousness but also practices that righteousness.

12. How can the breastplate of righteousness protect a believer from Satan?

_____
_____
_____
_____
_____

13. What do you need to do to better bind on both aspects of God's righteousness—right relationship to God and right action toward man?

_____
_____
_____
_____
_____
_____

THE SHOES OF PEACE

The shoes the Roman soldier wore in battle were spiked to enable him to plant his feet firmly in the ground. Some Christians tend to slip because their feet are not firmly planted. They are not making use of the proper equipment. Just as the track star uses spiked shoes to run his race, so does the Christian need the gospel of peace to race with a firm foothold. But what is meant by "the readiness that comes from the gospel of peace?" It means that solid grounding in the good news of peace with God gives the believer peace within himself and prepares him to share that peace with others.

"Peace" is total wholeness within and between persons. God's peace has two aspects. The believer already possesses peace *with* God because he has responded to the gospel of peace. Man is at enmity with God (Romans 5:10), but God offers him a message of peace. When he receives Christ into his life, peace with God is established. That is when the believer receives his spiked shoes to do battle with Satan. If he fails to wear those shoes, he is neglecting the second aspect of God's peace—the peace *of* God. Notice the distinction as you answer the following questions.

14. a. How does a person receive peace *with* God (Romans 5:1)?

    _____

    _____

    b. In your own words, what does that peace guarantee (Romans 8:1)?

    _____

    _____

15. a. How can the believer experience the peace *of* God daily (Philippians 4:6-7)?

    _____

    _____

    b. Why does this action open him to God's peace?

    _____

    _____

    _____

c. What result does the peace *of* God produce (Philippians 4:7)?

16. How else can you help to let God's peace rule in your heart (Colossians 3:15-16)? Why does this action help?

When God's anger and judgment are removed from you, God removes your sin and guilt. That is when you experience peace *with* God. The devil cannot change this status. However, he will do everything possible to keep you from enjoying the peace *of* God, which defuses anxiety. The enemy enjoys keeping you anxious, but God wants to free you from emotional turbulence.

Now, once you have established peace with God and are daily experiencing the peace of God, it is essential that you share that message of peace with others.

17. Describe how Paul encourages the believer to be prepared to share the gospel (Colossians 4:5-6).

18. How does Peter instruct believers to be prepared (1 Peter 3:15-16)?

19. Read Romans 12:16-21. How else can you witness to the peace that is in you? How does the peace in you enable you to do this?

_____

_____

_____

_____

_____

The alert soldier is ready to do battle. But the soldier who is undressed and sleeping, with his shoes in the corner, his breastplate lying on the ground and his belt thrown over a chair, will be defenseless in an attack.

Therefore, Peter warns, "Be self-controlled and alert. Your enemy the devil prowls about like a roaring lion looking for someone to devour. Resist him, standing firm in the faith . . ." (1 Peter 5:8-9).

THE SHIELD OF FAITH

The Roman soldier's shield was not a small weapon. It measured four feet in length and two and one-half feet in width. Its purpose was to provide a wall of protection against the enemy's fiery arrows. Faith is "accepting God's Word as truth and acting upon it."[1]

20. Study the fifteen darts in your enemy's arsenal recorded in Galatians 5:19-21. Choose one of them, and describe how faith could extinguish it. (For instance, if you choose the dart of immorality, you might say, "I accept the fact that my body is the temple of the Holy Spirit. Therefore I'm going to keep it free from immorality (1 Corinthians 6:19). I will keep it pure by abstaining from all appearance of evil (1 Thessalonians 5:22), and by fleeing from youthful lusts (2 Timothy 2:22). This means that I will not indulge myself by looking at sexually suggestive magazines, TV, or films, nor will I read novels or other material which arouse my passion. I will respect the girl or boy I date, and not use that person as a mere object for my sexual gratification. I will be careful not

to indulge in off-color jokes. And I will plan to experience the full enjoyment of a sexual relationship within the boundaries of marriage, having committed myself to my mate for life.")

_____
_____
_____
_____
_____
_____
_____
_____
_____

THE HELMET OF SALVATION

The helmet protects the head, which sends signals to the rest of the body. If the head is damaged, the entire body is damaged. Today many states require cyclists to wear helmets because so many young people have suffered brain damage or death due to accidents.

Likewise, the devil attempts to afflict your mind with doubts and confusion. Recall how he approached Eve: "Did God really say, 'You must not eat from any tree in the garden'" (Genesis 3:1)?

The helmet of salvation refers to the assurance of your salvation. Paul clarifies this in his admonition to the Thessalonians: "But since we belong to the day, let us be self-controlled, putting on faith and love as a breastplate, and *the hope of salvation* as a helmet" (1 Thessalonians 5:8). All believers possess salvation, but they do not all have the assurance of their salvation. Perhaps because some sin has overtaken them, they believe they have committed the unpardonable sin and have lost their salvation. But such is not the case.

21. a. What did David lose when he sinned against God by adultery and murder (Psalm 51:12)?

_____

b. How does John assure believers that God has forgiven them through Jesus (1 John 5:13-14)?

_____

c. What promise does Jesus give to those who have trusted in him (John 10:27-29)?

_____

_____

The unpardonable sin was attributing Jesus' miracles to the power of Satan. So long as the Pharisees refused to recognize divine power, they could not repent and be forgiven. Therefore, if you desire to repent, by definition you have not committed the unpardonable sin.

THE SWORD OF THE WORD

Although you have often seen pictures of soldiers swinging long swords at enemies, the sword in this passage is a small, twenty-four-inch blade. This weapon was used in hand-to-hand combat. It was like a dagger. Paul is picturing a close encounter with our enemy; the word "struggle" in verse 12 refers to wrestling.

The apostle also selects an interesting Greek term for "the word of God." The most common term translated "word" is *logos*, which refers to both Christ (John 1:1,14) and the Scriptures (2 Timothy 4:2). But in this passage Paul uses the word *rema*, which refers to the spoken word. He probably chose this term because he wanted to emphasize the *use* of the Scriptures.

22. How did Jesus use the spoken word to defend himself against Satan (Luke 4:4-12)? (Note carefully to whom He addressed God's words.)

_____

_____

_____

23. If you are going to use the spoken word effectively, what three conditions must you meet?

Psalm 119:11 _____

_____

Psalm 119:97 _____

2 Timothy 2:15 _____

24. What will you do to make better use of what God says?

_____
_____
_____
_____
_____

The last weapon Paul mentions is prayer, the words spoken between God and man and inspired by the Spirit. Like the Scripture, prayer is both an offensive and a defensive weapon. It is the key that makes all of the other weapons effective.

PRAYER

The prayerless Christian is vulnerable to Satan's attack. He can have all the other weapons at his disposal, but without prayer they are useless. Even after Paul speaks about the specific weapons which make up the full armor of God, he asks his readers, "Pray also for me, that whenever I open my mouth, words may be given me so that I will fearlessly make known the mystery of the gospel, for which I am an ambassador in chains. Pray that I may declare it fearlessly, as I should" (Ephesians 6:19-20). Even though he was eager to use the spoken word, he needed the intercessory prayers of his brothers and sisters in Christ.

25. a. What does James promise concerning prayer (James 5:16)?

_____
_____

b. Describe the hindrance to effective praying he uncovers (James 4:3).

_____
_____

c. James 4:7 implies why prayer is crucial to resisting the enemy. Explain the connection between prayer and submission to God.

_____
_____
_____
_____

26. What does Ephesians 6:18-19 teach you about how you should pray? Name and explain at least four instructions.

_____
_____
_____
_____
_____
_____

27. The following chart may help you in your prayer life.

Date	What I pray for myself	Date	God's Answer

Date	What I pray for others	Date	God's Answer

The full armor of God is your greatest resource for all satanic attack. The battles are many and the enemy is strong, but you have a complete arsenal at your fingertips. At times you will be knocked down. But like the old warrior, you will testify that you are "...hard pressed on every side, but not crushed; perplexed, but not in despair; persecuted, but not abandoned; struck down, but not destroyed" (2 Corinthians 4:8-9).

You may carry around some battle scars, but that is to be expected. God has made it possible for you to enjoy the thrill of victory and to avoid the agony of defeat.

Whenever you are tempted to give up, remember, "the one who is in you [God's Holy Spirit] is greater than the one who is in the world [the devil]" (1 John 4:4).